AMERICAN JOURNAL

LIBRARY OF
CONGRESS

BOOKS BY TRACY K. SMITH

Poetry
The Body's Question
Duende
Life on Mars
Wade in the Water

Memoir
Ordinary Light

AMERICAN JOURNAL

FIFTY POEMS FOR OUR TIME

SELECTED AND WITH AN INTRODUCTION BY

TRACY K. SMITH

GRAYWOLF PRESS

IN ASSOCIATION WITH THE LIBRARY OF CONGRESS

Permission acknowledgments appear on pages 115–120.

This publication is made possible, in part, by the voters of Minnesota through a Minnesota State Arts Board Operating Support grant, thanks to a legislative appropriation from the arts and cultural heritage fund, and a grant from the Wells Fargo Foundation. Significant support has also been provided by Target, the McKnight Foundation, the Lannan Foundation, the Amazon Literary Partnership, and other generous contributions from foundations, corporations, and individuals. To these organizations and individuals we offer our heartfelt thanks.

Published by Graywolf Press, in association with the Library of Congress
250 Third Avenue North, Suite 600
Minneapolis, Minnesota 55401

www.graywolfpress.org

Published in the United States of America
Printed in Canada

ISBN 978-1-55597-838-9 (cloth)
ISBN 978-1-55597-815-0 (paper)

2 4 6 8 9 7 5 3 1
First Graywolf Printing, 2018

Library of Congress Control Number: 2018934515 (cloth), 2018934515 (paper)

Cover design: Kyle G. Hunter

Cover art: Upper left: *In 1993, Thomas Crawford's Statue of Freedom was removed by helicopter from the U.S. Capitol dome for restoration. Washington, D.C.*, by Carol Highsmith, 1993. Carol M. Highsmith Archive, Library of Congress, Prints and Photographs Division, LC-DIG-highsm-13969. Upper right: *Maria Gomez, 3466 2nd Ave., LA*, by Camilo José Vergara, 2003. Library of Congress, Prints & Photographs Division, LC-DIG-vrg-00309. Lower left: *Richard Ortiz is a migrant worker in Nipomo, California, where famous photographer Dorothea Lange took a photograph of the Migrant Mother, Florence Owens Thompson in the 1930s*, by Carol Highsmith, 2013. The Jon B. Lovelace Collection of California Photographs in Carol M. Highsmith's America Project, Library of Congress, Prints and Photographs Division, LC-DIG-highsm-25212. Lower right (top): *"Sno-cone" stand, New Orleans, Louisiana*, by Carol Highsmith, between 1980 and 2006. Carol M. Highsmith Archive, Library of Congress, Prints and Photographs Division, LC-DIG-highsm-13991. Lower right (bottom): *Aerial view of mountaintop removal, approaching Racine*, by Lyntha Scott Eiler, 1995. Coal River Folklife Collection (AFC 1999/008), Library of Congress, American Folklife Center.

CONTENTS

AMERICAN JOURNAL

This is why I love poems: they invite me to sit down and listen to a voice speaking thoughtfully and passionately about what it feels like to be alive. Usually the someone doing the talking—the poem's speaker—is a person I'd never get the chance to meet were it not for the poem. Because the distance between us is too great. Or because we are too unlike one another to ever feel this at ease face-to-face. Or maybe because the person talking to me never actually existed as anything other than a figment of a poet's imagination, a character invented for reasons I may not ever know. Even when that someone is the real-life poet speaking of things that have actually happened, there is something different—some new strength, vulnerability, or authority—that the poem fosters. This is why I love poems: they require me to sit still, listen deeply, and imagine putting myself in someone else's unfamiliar shoes. The world I return to when the poem is over seems fuller and more comprehensible as a result.

American Journal: Fifty Poems for Our Time is an offering for people who love poems the way I do. It is also an offering for those who love them in different ways, and those who don't yet know what their relationship with poetry will be. I hope there is even something here to please readers who, for whatever the reason, might feel themselves to be at odds with poetry. These fifty poems—culled from living American poets of different ages, backgrounds, and aesthetic approaches, and with different views of what it feels like to be alive—welcome you to listen and be surprised, amused, consoled. These poems invite you to remember something you once knew, to see something you've never seen, and to range from one set of concerns to another. For the time that you are reading them, and even after, these poems will collapse the distance between you and fifty different real or imagined people with fifty different outlooks on the human condition.

But how? How do poems capture the significant yet hard-to-describe events and feelings punctuating our lives, and our time?

Poems call upon sounds and silence to operate like music. They invoke vivid sensory images to make abstract feelings like love or anger or doubt feel solid and unmistakable. Like movies, poems slow time down or speed it up; they cross cut from one viewpoint to another as a way of discerning connections between unlikely things; they use line and stanza breaks to create suspense. Even the visual layout of words on the page is a device to help conduct a reader's movement through the encounter that is the poem. These and other tools help poems call our attention to moments when the ordinary nature of experience changes—when the things we think we know flare into brighter colors, starker contrasts, strange and intoxicating possibilities.

There's something else these fifty poems are up to. As the title *American Journal* suggests, they are contemplating what it feels like to live, work, love, strive, raise a family, and survive many kinds of loss in this vast and varied nation. The great poet Robert Hayden, from Detroit, Michigan, was the first African American to serve in the role now known as Poet Laureate of the United States. His final collection contains an extraordinary poem called "[American Journal]," which is written in the voice of an alien from outer space sent to earth to observe humankind. On this planet, the speaker finds himself most drawn to "the americans," whom he calls "this baffling multi people." He recognizes America as a land of contrasts and contradictions, a place still new, still reckoning with the implications of its history. While much of life

in this nation strikes him as strange, some of what he observes
people doing reaches him as familiar:

> like us they have created a veritable populace
> of machines that serve and soothe and pamper
> and entertain   we have seen their flags and
> foot prints on the moon   also the intricate
> rubbish left behind   a wastefully ingenious
> people   many it appears worship the Unknowable
> Essence   the same for them as for us

And some of it, he finds perplexing:

> america   as much a problem in metaphysics as
> it is a nation earthly entity an iota in our
> galaxy   an organism that changes even as i
> examine it   fact and fantasy never twice the
> same   so many variables

Like many poets, Hayden allows his poem's speaker to build upon
what may be the poet's own complicated relationship to his sub-
ject matter. This figure from another planet, who moves through
human society without ever being fully integrated into it or under-
stood by his peers, provides the poet with the occasion and the
means to explore the real-life experience of social alienation, of
being a part of—and yet also at times apart from—a larger group.

I'm drawn to Hayden's poem because it paints a loving yet critical
portrait of a nation in progress, and because it emphasizes the many
forms that Americanness takes. In borrowing its title, I'm hoping to
make space for new reports on the American experience in our time.

These fifty poems take up stories old and new, and traditions deeply rooted and newly arrived. They bear witness to the daily struggles and promises of community, as well as to the times when community eludes us. They celebrate us and the natural world, and bow in reverence to the mysterious unknown. They do this and, inevitably, a great deal more. I am also hoping that their courage, intimacy of address, and even the journey they collectively map out—a journey that encompasses consideration of place; reflections on family and individual identity; responses to the urgencies affecting our collective culture; and gestures of love, hope, and remembrance—might go some way toward making us, whoever and wherever we are, a little less alien to one another.

Tracy K. Smith
Princeton, New Jersey

I. THE SMALL TOWN OF MY YOUTH

Second Estrangement

Please raise your hand,
whomever else of you
has been a child,
lost, in a market
or a mall, without
knowing it at first, following
a stranger, accidentally
thinking he is yours,
your family or parent, even
grabbing for his hands,
even calling the word
you said then for "Father,"
only to see the face
look strangely down, utterly
foreign, utterly not the one
who loves you, you
who are a bird suddenly
stunned by the glass partitions
of rooms.
      How far
the world you knew, & tall,
& filled, finally, with strangers.

In Defense of Small Towns

When I look at it, it's simple, really. I hate life there. September,
once filled with animal deaths and toughened hay. And the smells

of fall were boiled-down beets and potatoes
or the farmhands' breeches smeared with oil and diesel

as they rode into town, dusty and pissed. The radio station
split time between metal and Tejano, and the only action

happened on Friday nights where the high school football team
gave everyone a chance at forgiveness. The town left no room

for novelty or change. The sheriff knew everyone's son and
     despite that,
we'd cruise up and down the avenues, switching between

brake and gearshift. We'd fight and spit chew into Big Gulp cups
and have our hearts broken nightly. In that town I learned

to fire a shotgun at nine and wring a chicken's neck
with one hand by twirling the bird and whipping it straight like
     a towel.

But I loved the place once. Everything was blonde and cracked
and the irrigation ditches stretched to the end of the earth.
     You could

ride on a bicycle and see clearly the outline of every leaf
or catch on the streets each word of a neighbor's argument.

Nothing could happen there and if I willed it, the place would
    have me
slipping over its rocks into the river with the sugar plant's steam

or signing papers at a storefront army desk, buttoned up
with medallions and a crew cut, eyeing the next recruits.

If I've learned anything, it's that I could be anywhere,
staring at a hunk of asphalt or listening to the clap of billiard balls

against each other in a bar and hear my name. Indifference now?
Some. I shook loose, but that isn't the whole story. The fact is

I'm still in love. And when I wake up, I watch my son yawn,
and my mind turns his upswept hair into cornstalks

at the edge of a field. Stillness is an acre, and his body
idles, deep like heavy machinery. I want to take him back there,

to the small town of my youth and hold the book of wildflowers
open for him, and look. I want him to know the colors of horses,

to run with a cattail in his hand and watch as its seeds
fly weightless as though nothing mattered, as though

the little things we tell ourselves about our pasts stay there,
rising slightly and just out of reach.

'N'em

They said to say goodnight
And not goodbye, unplugged
The TV when it rained. They hid
Money in mattresses
So to sleep on decisions.
Some of their children
Were not their children. Some
Of their parents had no birthdates.
They could sweat a cold out
Of you. They'd wake without
An alarm telling them to.
Even the short ones reached
Certain shelves. Even the skinny
Cooked animals too quick
To catch. And I don't care
How ugly one of them arrived,
That one got married
To somebody fine. They fed
Families with change and wiped
Their kitchens clean.
Then another century came.
People like me forgot their names.

Flat as a Flitter

The way you can crush a bug
or stomp drained cans of Schlitz out on the porch,

the bread when it won't rise,
the cake when it falls after the oven-door slams—

the old people had their way
to describe such things. "But what's a flitter?"

I always asked my granny. And she could never say.
"It's just a flitter. Well, it might be a fritter."

"Then why not say 'fritter'?"
"Shit, Melissa. Because the old people said 'flitter.'"

And she smacked the fried pie into the skillet,
and banged the skillet on the stove,

and shook and turned the pie
till it was on its way to burnt.

Flatter than a flitter, a mountain
when its top's blown off:

dynamited, shaved to the seam,
the spoil pushed into hollers, into streams,

the arsenic slurry caged behind a dam,
teetering above an elementary school.

The old people said "flitter." They didn't live to see
God's own mountain turned

hazard-orange mid-air pond,
a haze of waste whose brightness rivals heaven.

When that I was a little bitty baby,
my daddy drove up into Virginia

to fix strip-mining equipment, everything
to him an innocent machine in need.

On God's own mountain,
poor people drink bad water, and the heart

of the Lord is a seam of coal gouged out
to fuel the light in other places.

The old people didn't live
to give a name to this

kingdom of gravel and blast.
Lay me a hunk of coal

on my flittered tongue
to mark the mountains' graves,

to mark my father's tools
quarrying bread for my baby plate,

to mark my granny slapping dough
as if with God's own flat hand.

Sugar and Brine: Ella's Understanding

Daddy slaughtered the hog right there in the side yard,
and it hurt to see it, but that won't stop me from eating.
Come Thanksgiving, I'll dip a bit of ham in Jackson's
Ribbon Cane Syrup, and pop it inside a biscuit.
When it's time to celebrate, something dies.
When something dies, we take it with the sweet.

Take my cousin Gerald—he left us last summer,
a tractor accident. We were cousins by marriage, but
friends by choice, so I cried more than when I broke my leg
jumping off the front porch—bone snapped clean through.
After the funeral, as the Lord is my witness,
those were the best potato pies I ever had.

Yesterday, where the yellow pines meet the creek,
that boy on the other side of the property line
helped bring his daddy's cattle in. I watched him watch
me standing in a field littered with cow's corn,
my head tilted just enough to let him know I was
curious. He left a scarlet ribbon tied to the barbed wire.
My heart skipped quicker than a swallow's when I found it.
Now I'm wondering what throat's going to open?
I need to warn him—the wheel never rusts, never stops.

The Field Trip

This time they're thirteen, no longer
interested in the trillium on the path but in each other,
though they will not say so. Only the chaperone
lingers at the adder's-tongue,
watching the teacher trail the rest uphill
to where the dense virginal forest thins and opens.
At the clearing, she tells them to be still and mute
and make a list of what they see and hear.
A girl asks if she should also list
the way she feels—she's the one
who'll cite the shadow on the lake below.
The others sprawl on gender-separate rocks
except for the smart-ass, perched
on the cliff-edge, inviting front-page photos—
PICNIC MARRED BY TRAGEDY. From time to time,
in the midst of the day's continual lunch,
as the students read the lists their teacher edits,
the boy swears and stretches—
he is in fact fourteen, doing seventh grade
a second time, this same assignment
also a second time. Pressed, he says
he sees exactly what he saw before—ponds, rocks, trees—
shouting it back from the same vantage point
out on the twelve-inch ledge,
Long Pond a ragged puddle underneath him;
and what he shouts grows more and more
dangerously insubordinate as he leans

more and more dramatically over the edge.
But he is, after all, the first to spot the hawk;
and it is, looking down on it, amazing. The others
gather near the unimpeded view,
together, finally, standing on this bluff
overlooking three natural ponds, hearing the wind
ruffle the cedar fringe, watching the hawk
float along the thermals like a leaf.
And for a moment, belittled by indifferent wilderness,
you want to praise the boy, so much does he resemble
if not the hawk then the doomed shrub
fanned against the rockface there beside him,
rooted in a fissure in the rock.
But soon the hero swings back up to earth,
the group divides. Just like that
they're ready for home, tired of practicing:
sixteen children, two adults, and one
bad boy who carved a scorpion on his arm.

Mighty Pawns

If I told you Earl, the toughest kid
on my block in North Philadelphia,
bow-legged and ominous, could beat
any man or woman in ten moves playing white,
or that he traveled to Yugoslavia to frustrate the bearded
masters at the Belgrade Chess Association,
you'd think I was given to hyperbole,
and if, at dinnertime, I took you
into the faint light of his Section 8 home
reeking of onions, liver, and gravy,
his six little brothers fighting on a broken love-seat
for room in front of a cracked flat-screen,
one whose diaper sags it's a wonder
it hasn't fallen to his ankles,
the walls behind doors exposing sheetrock
the perfect O of a handle, and the slats
of stairs missing where Baby-boy gets stuck
trying to ascend to a dominion foreign to you and me
with its loud timbales and drums blasting down
from the closed room of his cousin whose mother
stands on a corner on the other side of town
all times of day and night, except when her relief
check arrives at the beginning of the month,
you'd get a better picture of Earl's ferocity
after-school on the board in Mr. Sherman's class,
but not necessarily when he stands near you
at a downtown bus-stop in a jacket a size too

19

small, hunching his shoulders around his ears,
as you imagine the checkered squares of his poverty
and anger, and pray he does not turn his precise gaze
too long in your direction for fear he blames
you and proceeds to take your Queen.

FROM *summer, somewhere*

somewhere, a sun. below, boys brown
as rye play the dozens & ball, jump

in the air & stay there. boys become new
moons, gum-dark on all sides, beg bruise

-blue water to fly, at least tide, at least
spit back a father or two. i won't get started.

history is what it is. it knows what it did.
bad dog. bad blood. bad day to be a boy

color of a July well spent. but here, not earth
not heaven, we can't recall our white shirts

turned ruby gowns. here, there's no language
for *officer* or *law*, no color to call *white*.

if snow fell, it'd fall black. please, don't call
us dead, call us alive someplace better.

we say our own names when we pray.
we go out for sweets & come back.

Walking Home

Everything dies, I said. How had that started?

A tree? The winter? Not me, she said.

And I said, Oh yeah? And she said, I'm reincarnating.

Ha, she said, See you in a few thousand years!

Why years, I wondered, why not minutes? Days?

She found that so funny—Ha Ha—doubled over—

Years, she said, confidently.

I think you and I have known each other a few lifetimes, I said.

She said, I have never before been a soul on this earth.

(It was cold. We were hungry.) Next time, you be the mother,
    I said.

No way, Jose, she said, as we turned the last windy corner.

Music from Childhood

You grow up hearing two languages. Neither fits your fits
Your mother informs you "moon" means "window to another
  world."

You begin to hear words mourn the sounds buried inside their
  mouths
A row of yellow windows and a painting of them

Your mother informs you "moon" means "window to another
  world."
You decide it is better to step back and sit in the shadows

A row of yellow windows and a painting of them
Someone said you can see a blue pagoda or a red rocket ship

You decide it is better to step back and sit in the shadows
Is it because you saw a black asteroid fly past your window

Someone said you can see a blue pagoda or a red rocket ship
I tried to follow in your footsteps, but they turned to water

Is it because I saw a black asteroid fly past my window
The air hums—a circus performer riding a bicycle towards the
  ceiling

I tried to follow in your footsteps, but they turned to water
The town has started sinking back into its commercial

The air hums—a circus performer riding a bicycle towards the
    ceiling
You grow up hearing two languages. Neither fits your fits

The town has started sinking back into its commercial
You begin to hear words mourn the sounds buried inside their
    mouths

Girls Overheard While Assembling a Puzzle

Are you sure this blue is the same as the
blue over there? This wall's like the
bottom of a pool, its
color I mean. I need a
darker two-piece this summer, the kind with
elastic at the waist so it actually
fits. I can't
find her hands. Where does this gold
go? It's like the angel's giving
her a little piece of honeycomb to eat.
I don't see why God doesn't
just come down and
kiss her himself. This is the red of that
lipstick we saw at the
mall. This piece of her
neck could fit into the light part
of the sky. I think this is a
piece of water. What kind of
queen? You mean
right here? And are we supposed to believe
she can suddenly
talk angel? Who thought this stuff
up? I wish I had a
velvet bikini. That flower's the color of the
veins in my grandmother's hands. I
wish we could

walk into that garden and pick an
X-ray to float on.
Yeah. I do too. I'd say a
zillion yeses to anyone for that.

Passing

At a station in a no-name town,
a blue-red coleus

blooms from a cleft in the track.
Too obvious, I say, out loud

to the window, to God,
to no one, rolling my white eyes

into my thick bright head.
If I arrive,

who will greet me as brother,
as owner, who will greet me

at all, feeling from my veins
the pull of our one long pulse—

Pissing into the metal bin, my waste
streaming out onto the track,

I laugh at the mirror, an animal,
unhinging, trying

to see what they see
in whatever I am standing here—Then

the train slides into a long tunnel.
The lights flicker off

and I am back inside my mother.

II. SOMETHING SHINES OUT FROM EVERY DARKNESS

"Let me tell you about my marvelous god"

Let me tell you about my marvelous god, how he hides in the
    hexagons
of the bees, how the drought that wrings its leather hands
above the world is of his making, as well as the rain in the quiet
    minutes
that leave only thoughts of rain.
An atom is working and working, an atom is working in deepest
night, then bursting like the farthest star; it is far
smaller than a pinprick, far smaller than a zero and it has no
will, no will toward us.
This is why the heart has paced and paced,
will pace and pace across the field where yarrow
was and now is dust. A leaf catches
in a bone. The burrow's shut by a tumbled clod
and the roots, upturned, are hot to the touch.
How my god is a feathered and whirling thing; you will singe
    your arm
when you pluck him from the air,
when you pluck him from that sky
where sorrow swirls, and you will burn again
throwing him back.

Sister as Moving Object

my sister is moving in me again
with her long   arms and legs

moving to tell me   she's still here
inside my body   along with fireballs

free-roaming breath   some days she's a tanker truck
magnetic   gleaming down my highways

some days   an ocean liner   splitting
the dark waters   today   my sister's particular beauty

rocks the house   to 1965   wearing pink-pink-
caked-on lipstick   tight pants   teased-up-

Ann-Margaret hair   could've been anyone's
sister and was   adopted from another place

she raised me up   taught me   the necessary things:
how to mix   water with bourbon   in the picture-frame bar

how to mix   the real and the unreal   and make it glisten
sea of submerged heartache   great blanket of sea:

seamount   *sweptback*   *from the guyot to the springboard*
sluice   *railbed*   *heart of copper field*

nightshade   when she hid her arsonist boyfriend
in the basement closet   (when the cops came looking for him)

she taught me the power of a lie: *no, I haven't seen him*
no, not since yesterday   she taught me to be visible   then follow

the circle down: *ball bearings*   *axehandles*
fields of snakes   hot spur of escape   when she ran downstairs

to tip him off: *now! through the backyards*
they won't look there   she gave and gave   early lessons in desire

her and her dark haired muscle boy   on the rock
behind the shopping center   me the lookout   air thick

with everything coming   his thin teeshirt   i watched their mouths:
|torrential| everything i wanted   moving through them

today I name the lasting roads: *artery   toll road   road of disguise*
she taught me imprisonment   not being a rat:

I took to the heat   like a dog to an electric fence   don't go past
the edge of the yard   2 girls blank from no beginnings   in combat

so tall   the only way to beat her   was to scissor her
between my thick legs   and squeeze

tonight   the house humming   her particular beauty:
lack of compromise   she grabbed the nail scissors   stabbed me:

33

sea of the head thrown back   she, later   dancing to loud music
said: *do it like this, don't listen*   *to what they tell you*

sea we never shared   blood sea

FROM *The Split*

1. She was starting to look like her mother.
2. She was clingier than pantyhose.
3. He stayed out all night.
4. She liked to cuff me when she got plowed.
5. He was vapid.
6. She was a fool.
7. She ridiculed me in front of the dogs.
8. He stuck a hairpin in my ear.
9. He had an affair with my older sister.
10. He spent our money on booze and bennies.
11. She wouldn't clean and it stank like bad beef.
12. I tried to hang myself but it didn't work.
13. He didn't like my sweet potato pie and said his mother made it better.
14. She wouldn't learn trigonometry for me.
15. I took it all out on the little ones.
16. She couldn't get pregnant.
17. He was shooting blanks.
18. He made for a pitiful sight in a bathing suit.
19. I wanted out, then I didn't, then I did.
20. I just couldn't live without Sally.
21. He wanted to start a family and to start it now, with me.
22. She split when the money ran out.
23. I gave her three more chances and then I left.
24. She hated the Dave Clark Five.
25. I was indentured. I didn't know I could choose not to.
26. He went out for gum etcetera.

27. By April she had passed on.
28. He saw only his idea of me.
29. We couldn't agree on an invitation font.
30. He was bad news, and it's always, like, *bad news, here I am.*

The Hypno-Domme Speaks, and Speaks and Speaks

I was born as a woman, I talk you to death,
        or else your ear off,
or else you to sleep. What do I have, all the time
in the world, and a voice that swings brass back
and forth, you can hear it, and a focal point where
my face should be. What do I have, I have absolute
power, and what I want is your money, your drool,
and your mind, and the sense of myself as a snake,
and a garter in the grass. Every bone in the snake
is the hipbone, every part of the snake is the hips.
The first sound I make is silence, then sssssshhh,
    the first word I say is listen. Sheep shearers
      and accountants hypnotize the hardest,
and lookout sailors who watch the sea, and the boys
who cut and cut and cut and cut and cut the grass.
The writers who write page-turners, and the writers
who repeat themselves. The diamond-cutter kneels
down before me and asks me to hypnotize him, and
I glisten at him and glisten hard, and listen to me and
listen, I tell him. Count your age backward, I tell him.
Become aware of your breathing, and aware of mine
       which will go on longer. Believe you
    are a baby till I tell you otherwise, then believe
you're a man till I tell you you're dirt. When a gunshot
rings out you'll lie down like you're dead. When you
    hear, "He is breathing," you'll stand up again.
The best dog of the language is Yes and protects you.

The best black-and-white dog of the language is Yes
and goes wherever you go, and you go where I say,
you go anywhere. Why do I do it is easy, I am working
my way through school. Give me the money
                           for Modernism, and give me the money
for what comes next. When you wake to the fact that you
have a body, you will wake to the fact that not for long.
When you wake you will come when you read the word
hard, or hard to understand me, or impenetrable poetry.
When you put down the book you will come when you
hear the words put down the book,
                           you will come when you hear.

The Poet at Fifteen
after Larry Levis

You wear faded black
and paint your face white as the blessed
teeth of Jesus
because brown isn't high art
unless you are a beautiful savage.

All the useless tautologies—

This is me. I am this. I am me.

In your ragged
Salvation Army sweaters, in your brilliant

awkwardness. White dresses
like Emily Dickinson.

I dreaded that first Robin,
so, at fifteen you slash
your wrists.

You're not allowed
to shave your legs in the hospital.

The atmosphere
that year: sometimes you exist
and sometimes you think you're Mrs. Dalloway.

This is bold—existing.

You do not understand your parents
who understand you less:
your father who listens to ABBA after work,
your mother who eats expired food.

How do you explain what you have done?
With your hybrid mouth, a split tongue.

How do you explain the warmth
sucking you open, leaving you
like a gutted machine?

It is a luxury to tell a story.

How do you explain
that the words are made by more
than your wanting?

Te chingas o te jodes.

At times when you speak Spanish, your tongue
is flaccid inside your rotten mouth:

desgraciada, sin vergüenza.

At the hospital they're calling your name
with an accent on the *E*. They bring you
tacos, a tiny golden crucifix.

Your father has run
all the way from the factory.

My Brother at 3 AM

He sat cross-legged, weeping on the steps
when Mom unlocked and opened the front door.
    O God, he said, *O God*.
        He wants to kill me, Mom.

When Mom unlocked and opened the front door
at 3 a.m., she was in her nightgown, Dad was asleep.
    He wants to kill me, he told her,
        looking over his shoulder.

3 a.m. and in her nightgown, Dad asleep,
What's going on? she asked, *Who wants to kill you?*
    He looked over his shoulder.
        The devil does. Look at him, over there.

She asked, *What are you on? Who wants to kill you?*
The sky wasn't black or blue but the green of a dying night.
    The devil, look at him, over there.
        He pointed to the corner house.

The sky wasn't black or blue but the dying green of night.
Stars had closed their eyes or sheathed their knives.
    My brother pointed to the corner house.
        His lips flickered with sores.

Stars had closed their eyes or sheathed their knives.
O God, I can see the tail, he said. *O God, look.*
    Mom winced at the sores on his lips.
        It's sticking out from behind the house.

O God, see the tail, he said. *Look at the goddamned tail.*
He sat cross-legged, weeping on the front steps.
    Mom finally saw it, a hellish vision, my brother.
        O God, O God, she said.

Reverse Suicide

The guy Dad sold your car to
comes back to get his money,

leaves the car. With filthy rags
we rub it down until it doesn't shine

and wipe your blood into
the seams of the seat.

Each snowflake stirs before
lifting into the sky as I

learn you won't be dead.
The unsuffering ends

when the mess of your head
pulls together around

a bullet in your mouth.
You spit it into Dad's gun

before arriving in the driveway
while the evening brightens

and we pour bag after bag
of leaves on the lawn,

waiting for them to leap
onto the bare branches.

Charlottesville Nocturne

The late September night is a train of thought, a wound
That doesn't bleed, dead grass that's still green,
No off-shoots, no elegance,
                              the late September night,
Deprived of adjectives, abstraction's utmost and gleam.

It has been said there is an end to the giving out of names.
It has been said that everything that's written has grown hollow.
It has been said that scorpions dance where language falters and
    gives way.
It has been said that something shines out from every darkness,
                              that something shines out.

Leaning against the invisible, we bend and nod.
Evening arranges itself around the fallen leaves
Alphabetized across the backyard,
                              desolate syllables
That braille us and sign us, leaning against the invisible.

Our dreams are luminous, a cast fire upon the world.
Morning arrives and that's it.
                    Sunlight darkens the earth.

Downhearted

Six horses died in a tractor-trailer fire.
There. That's the hard part. I wanted
to tell you straight away so we could
grieve together. So many sad things,
that's just one on a long recent list
that loops and elongates in the chest,
in the diaphragm, in the alveoli. What
is it they say, *heartsick* or *downhearted*?
I picture a heart lying down on the floor
of the torso, pulling up the blankets
over its head, thinking this pain will
go on forever (even though it won't).
The heart is watching Lifetime movies
and wishing, and missing all the good
parts of her that she has forgotten.
The heart is so tired of beating
herself up, she wants to stop it still,
but also she wants the blood to return,
wants to bring in the thrill and wind of the ride,
the fast pull of life driving underneath her.
What the heart wants? The heart wants
her horses back.

becoming a horse

It was dragging my hands along its belly,
loosing the bit and wiping the spit
from its mouth made me
a snatch of grass in the thing's maw,
a fly tasting its ear. It was
touching my nose to his made me know
the clover's bloom, my wet eye to his
made me know the long field's secrets.
But it was putting my heart to the horse's that made me know
the sorrow of horses. The sorrow
of a brook creasing a field. The maggot
turning in its corpse. Made me
forsake my thumbs for the sheen of unshod hooves.
And in this way drop my torches.
And in this way drop my knives.
Feel the small song in my chest
swell and my coat glisten and twitch.
And my face grow long.
And these words cast off, at last,
for the slow honest tongue of horses.

After the Diagnosis

No remembering now
when the apple sapling was blown
almost out of the ground.
No telling how,
with all the other trees around,
it alone was struck.
It must have been luck,
he thought for years, so close
to the house it grew.
It must have been night.
Change is a thing one sleeps through
when young, and he was young.
If there was a weakness in the earth,
a give he went down on his knees
to find and feel the limits of,
there is no longer.
If there was one random blow from above
the way he's come to know
from years in this place,
the roots were stronger.
Whatever the case,
he has watched this tree survive
wind ripping at his roof for nights
on end, heats and blights
that left little else alive.
No remembering now . . .
A day's changes mean all to him

and all days come down
to one clear pane
through which he sees
among all the other trees
this leaning, clenched, unyielding one
that seems cast
in the form of a blast
that would have killed it,
as if something at the heart of things,
and with the heart of things,
had willed it.

Heart/mind

A bear batting at a beehive, how

clumsy the mind
always was with the heart. Wanting
what it wanted.

The blizzard's
accountant, how
timidly the heart approached the business
of the mind. Counting
what it counted.

Light inside a cage, the way the heart—

Bird trapped in an airport, the way the mind—

How it flashed on the floor of the phone booth, my
last dime. And

this letter
I didn't send
how surprising

to find it now.

All this love I must have felt.

III. WORDS TANGLED IN DEBRIS

Who's Who

You wake up from a nap.
Your mouth feels like a cheap acrylic sweater.
You blink online and 3-D images hopscotch around you.
A telenovela actress hides under your lampshade.
You switch to voice activation.
Good Afternoon! Sings the voice of Gregory Peck.
You look out your window, across the street.
Faded mattresses sag against a chain-link fence.
The mattress seller sits on a crate, clipping his fingernails.
You think of inviting him in.
You do a scan.
Gregory Peck booms: Dwayne Healey, 28, convicted felon of
    petty larceny.
You don't know what to do so you pet your ceramic cat.
What? You ask. What? You want to go out? Well you can't.
You hear a chime.
It is your former employer informing you that they cannot release
your husband's password due to the Privacy Policy.
It is the 98th auto reply.
You bite your hand.
You check in on your husband.
After your husband went on roam, you received one message
    from him:
I am by a pond and a coyote is eating a frog. It's amazing.
You decide to go outside.
You walk to the public park.

There is a track where people run while watching whatever
they're watching.
You sit on an oversized bench.
You think of your old town house with the oatmeal sofa
before you and husband downgraded to this neighborhood.
The sofa made you happy.
You decide you need to keep up appearances.
You need to clip your husband's nails. They are getting long.
A strangled *yip* escapes from you and a jogger stares at you.
You see a palm tree and it is carved up with little penis drawings.
You make a sound like tut-tut.
You enhance the park.
You fill in the balding grass and rub the offensive drawings
from the tree. You add coconuts.
You feel your insides are being squeezed out through a tiny hole
the size of a mosquito bite.
You hear children laughing as they rush out of a bus and it sounds
far away and watery, like how it used to in the movies, when the
    light was haloey,
and it was slow-motion, and the actor was having a terrible
    flashback.
But you are not having a flashback.
Underneath the sound of children laughing, you hear users
    chatting
over each other, which all blurs into a warring shadow of insects
and the one that sounds like a hornet is your husband,
telling you to put his stuff in storage.
Or sell it to pay off bills or
leave, why don't you goddamn leave.

You sit on the bench until the sky turns pink.
When your former employer let you go,
they said, you are now free to pursue what you want to pursue.
So here you are.

Minimum Wage

My mother and I are on the front porch lighting each other's
    cigarettes
as if we were on a ten-minute break from our jobs
at being a mother and son, just ten minutes
to steal a moment of freedom before clocking back in, before
putting the aprons back on, the paper hats,
washing our hands twice and then standing
behind the counter again,
hoping for tips, hoping the customers
will be nice, will say some kind word, the cool
front yard before us and the dogs
in the backyard shitting on everything.
We are hunched over, two extras on the set of *The Night of
    the Hunter.*
I am pulling a second cigarette out of the pack, a swimmer
rising from a pool of other swimmers. Soon we will go back
inside and sit in the yellow kitchen and drink
the rest of the coffee
and what is coming to kill us will pour milk
into mine and sugar into hers.

Proximities

A man walks into a coffee shop.
But it's not a joke.
I bought coffee there
last summer.
Small, with milk.
It's never a joke
to walk in or out of a shop
unharmed. It's easy
to forget
you aren't a person
being shot at.
I'm not.
I wasn't, though
I was there
last summer.
Not-shot-at
and I never knew it.
Did not once
think it.
Thinking it now
the moment thins,
it sheers
and I move back
to other coffee shops
where I never fell, or bled,
and then

I sit for a while
with my regular cup
and feel things collapse
or go on, I can't tell.

Story of Girls

Years ago, my brothers took turns holding down a girl in a room.
They weren't doing anything to her but they were laughing and
sometimes it's the laughing that does enough. They held the girl
   down

for an hour and she was crying, her mouth stuffed with a small
   red cloth.
Their laughing matched her crying in the same pitch. That marriage
of sound was an error and the error kept repeating itself.

There were threats of putting her in the closet or in the basement
if she didn't quiet down. One cousin told them to stop but no
   one could
hear him above the high roar. After that the boy was silent,
   looking down

at his hands, gesturing toward the locked door. The mother was
   able
to push the door in and the boys were momentarily ashamed,
   remembering
for the first time that the girl was their younger sister. The
   mother ran

to the girl fearful that something had been damaged. Nothing
   was touched.
The brothers were merely dismissed as they jostled each other
   down

the long staircase. The girl sat up to breathe a little, then a little
more.

Oftentimes it's the quiet cousin I think about.

Fourth Grade Autobiography

We live in Los Angeles, California.
We have a front yard and a backyard.
My favorite things are cartwheels, salted plums,
and playing catch with my dad. I squeeze the grass
and dirt between my fingers. Eat my tongue
white. He launches every ball into orbit.
Every ball drops like an anvil, heavy
and straight into my hands. I am afraid
of riots and falling and the dark.
The sunset of flames ringing our block,
groceries and Asian-owned storefronts. No one
to catch me. Midnight walks from his room to mine.
I believe in the devil.
I have a sister and a brother
and a strong headlock. We have a dog named
Spunky, fawn and black. We have an olive
tree. A black walnut tree. A fig tree.
We lie in the grass and wonder who writes
in the sky. I lie in the grass and imagine
my name, a cloud drifting. Saturday
dance parties. Everyone drunk on pink
panties, screw drivers, and Canadian Club.
Dominoes and spades. Al Green and Mack 10.
Sometimes Mama dances with the dog.
Sometimes my dad dances with me. I am
careful not to touch. He is careful
to smile with his whole face.

No

Yes, that was me you saw shaking with bravery, with a
government-issued rifle on my back. I'm sorry I could not
greet you, as you deserved, my relative.

They were not my tears. I have a reservoir inside. They will
be cried by my sons, my daughters if I can't learn how to
turn tears to stone.

Yes, that was me, standing in the back door of the house in
the alley, with fresh corn and bread for the neighbors.

I did not foresee the flood of blood. How they would forget
our friendship, would return to kill the babies and me.

Yes, that was me whirling on the dance floor. We made such
a racket with all that joy. I loved the whole world in that silly
music.

I did not realize the terrible dance in the staccato of bullets.

Yes. I smelled the burning grease of corpses. And like a fool
I expected our words might rise up and jam the artillery in
the hands of dictators.

We had to keep going. We sang our grief to clean the air of
turbulent spirits.

Yes, I did see the terrible black clouds as I cooked dinner. And the messages of the dying spelled there in the ashy sunset. Every one addressed: "mother."

There was nothing about it in the news. Everything was the same. Unemployment was up. Another queen crowned with flowers. Then there were the sports scores.

Yes, the distance was great between your country and mine. Yet our children played in the path between our houses.

No. We had no quarrel with each other.

The Long Deployment

For weeks, I breathe his body in the sheet
        and pillow. I lift a blanket to my face.
There's bitter incense paired with something sweet,
        like sandalwood left sitting in the heat
or cardamom rubbed on a piece of lace.
        For weeks, I breathe his body. In the sheet
I smell anise, the musk that we secrete
        with longing, leather and moss. I find a trace
of bitter incense paired with something sweet.
        Am I imagining the wet scent of peat
and cedar, oud, impossible to erase?
        For weeks, I breathe his body in the sheet—
crushed pepper—although perhaps discreet,
        difficult for someone else to place.
There's bitter incense paired with something sweet.
        With each deployment I become an aesthete
of smoke and oak. Patchouli fills the space
        for weeks. I breathe his body in the sheet
until he starts to fade, made incomplete,
        a bottle almost empty in its case.
There's bitter incense paired with something sweet.
        And then he's gone. Not even the conceit
of him remains, not the resinous base.
        For weeks, I breathed his body in the sheet.
He was bitter incense paired with something sweet.

FROM *Personal Effects*

Daily I sit
with the language
they've made

of our language

to NEUTRALIZE
the CAPABILITY of LOW DOLLAR VALUE ITEMS
like you.

You are what is referred to as
a "CASUALTY." Unclear whether
from a CATALYTIC or FRONTAL ATTACK, unclear

the final time you were addressed

thou, beloved. It was for us a
CATASTROPHIC EVENT.

Just, DESTROYED.

DIED OF WOUND RECEIVED IN ACTION.

Yes, there was
EARLY WARNING.
You said you were especially scared
of mortar rounds.

In EXECUTION PLANNING, they weighed
the losses, the SUSTAINABILITY
and budgeted

for X number,
they budgeted for the phone call
to your mother and weighed that

against the amount saved in rations
and your taste for cigarettes

and the tea you poured your boys
and the tea you would've poured me
approaching *Hello.*

The change you collected in jars
jumping a bit
as the family learns to slam
the home's various doors.

We Lived Happily during the War

And when they bombed other people's houses, we

protested
but not enough, we opposed them but not

enough. I was
in my bed, around my bed America

was falling: invisible house by invisible house by invisible house.

I took a chair outside and watched the sun.

In the sixth month
of a disastrous reign in the house of money

in the street of money in the city of money in the country of money,
our great country of money, we (forgive us)

lived happily during the war.

Phantom Noise

There is this ringing hum   this
bullet-borne language   ringing
shell-fall and static this   late-night
ringing of threadwork and carpet   ringing
hiss and steam   this wing-beat
of rotors and tanks   broken
bodies ringing in steel   humming these
voices of dust   these years ringing
rifles in Babylon   rifles in Sumer
ringing these children their gravestones
and candy   their limbs gone missing   their
static-borne television   their ringing
this eardrum   this rifled symphonic   this
ringing of midnight in gunpowder and oil   this
brake pad gone useless   this muzzle-flash singing   this
threading of bullets in muscle and bone   this ringing
hum   this ringing hum   this
ringing

Ten Drumbeats to God

I confess to stealing the tomb to bury my mother. I admit to emptying the gas tank my neighbor kept for *blakawout*. I took the rope and the cakes of an old lady because she had more and I needed some. I stole a radio to eat. Stole medicine to sleep. I tried to forget I lay beside dead bodies but my eyes couldn't shut. Tried to refill my heart but it stayed shut. I wished and wish some more to be dead and not an idea, a solitude, a shame. I summoned words tangled in debris, measured the distance of fire a mile into my voice. I took everything and a little more. Then I heard the drumbeats and remembered—like rain like song like light lit by old questions—there is no reason, there is god, drum, beat. there is what lingers and there is what comes later.

IV. HERE,
THE SENTENCE WILL BE RESPECTED

38

Here, the sentence will be respected.

I will compose each sentence with care, by minding what the rules of writing dictate.

For example, all sentences will begin with capital letters.

Likewise, the history of the sentence will be honored by ending each one with appropriate punctuation such as a period or question mark, thus bringing the idea to (momentary) completion.

You may like to know, I do not consider this a "creative piece."

I do not regard this as a poem of great imagination or a work of fiction.

Also, historical events will not be dramatized for an "interesting" read.

Therefore, I feel most responsible to the orderly sentence; conveyor of thought.

That said, I will begin.

You may or may not have heard about the Dakota 38.

If this is the first time you've heard of it, you might wonder, "What is the Dakota 38?"

The Dakota 38 refers to thirty-eight Dakota men who were executed by hanging, under orders from President Abraham Lincoln.

To date, this is the largest "legal" mass execution in US history.

The hanging took place on December 26, 1862—the day after Christmas.

This was the *same week* that President Lincoln signed the Emancipation Proclamation.

In the preceding sentence, I italicize "same week" for emphasis.

There was a movie titled *Lincoln* about the presidency of Abraham Lincoln.

The signing of the Emancipation Proclamation was included in the film *Lincoln*; the hanging of the Dakota 38 was not.

In any case, you might be asking, "Why were the thirty-eight Daktoa men hung?"

As a side note, the past tense of hang is *hung*, but when referring to the capital punishment of hanging, the correct past tense is *hanged*.

So it's possible that you're asking, "Why were thirty-eight Dakota men hanged?"

They were hanged for the Sioux Uprising.

I want to tell you about the Sioux Uprising, but I don't know where to begin.

I may jump around and details will not unfold in chronological order.

Keep in mind, I am not a historian.

So I will recount facts as best as I can, given limited resources and understanding.

Before Minnesota was a state, the Minnesota region, generally speaking, was the traditional homeland for Dakota, Anishinaabeg, and Ho-Chunk people.

During the 1800s, when the US expanded territory, they "purchased" land from the Dakota people as well as the other tribes.

But another way to understand that sort of "purchase" is: Dakota leaders ceded land to the US government in exchange for money or goods, but most importantly, the safety of their people.

Some say that Dakota leaders did not understand the terms they were entering, or they never would have agreed.

Even others call the entire negotiation "trickery."

But to make whatever-it-was official and binding, the US government drew up an initial treaty.

This treaty was later replaced by another (more convenient) treaty, and then another.

I've had difficulty unraveling the terms of these treaties, given the legal speak and congressional language.

As treaties were abrogated (broken) and new treaties were drafted, one after another, the new treaties often referenced old defunct treaties, and it is a muddy, switchback trail to follow.

Although I often feel lost on this trail, I know I am not alone.

However, as best as I can put the facts together, in 1851, Dakota territory was contained to a twelve-mile by one-hundred-fifty-mile-long strip along the Minnesota River.

But just seven years later, in 1858, the northern portion was ceded (taken) and the southern portion was (conveniently) allotted, which reduced Dakota land to a stark ten-mile tract.

These amended and broken treaties are often referred to as the Minnesota Treaties.

The word *Minnesota* comes from *mni*, which means water; and *sota*, which means turbid.

Synonyms for turbid include muddy, unclear, cloudy, confused, and smoky.

Everything is in the language we use.

For example, a treaty is, essentially, a contract between two sovereign nations.

The US treaties with the Dakota Nation were legal contracts that promised money.

It could be said, this money was payment for the land the Dakota ceded; for living within assigned boundaries (a reservation); and for relinquishing rights to their vast hunting territory which, in turn, made Dakota people dependent on other means to survive: money.

The previous sentence is circular, akin to many aspects of history.

As you may have guessed by now, the money promised in the turbid treaties did not make it into the hands of Dakota people.

In addition, local government traders would not offer credit to "Indians" to purchase food or goods.

Without money, store credit, or rights to hunt beyond their ten-mile tract of land, Dakota people began to starve.

The Dakota people were starving.

The Dakota people starved.

In the preceding sentence, the word "starved" does not need italics for emphasis.

One should read "The Dakota people starved" as a straightforward and plainly stated fact.

As a result—and without other options but to continue to starve—Dakota people retaliated.

Dakota warriors organized, struck out, and killed settlers and traders.

This revolt is called the Sioux Uprising.

Eventually, the US Cavalry came to Mnisota to confront the Uprising.

More than one thousand Dakota people were sent to prison.

As already mentioned, thirty-eight Dakota men were subsequently hanged.

After the hanging, those one thousand Dakota prisoners were released.

However, as further consequence, what remained of Dakota territory in Mnisota was dissolved (stolen).

The Dakota people had no land to return to.

This means they were exiled.

Homeless, the Dakota people of Mnisota were relocated (forced) onto reservations in South Dakota and Nebraska.

Now, every year, a group called the Dakota 38 + 2 Riders conduct a memorial horse ride from Lower Brule, South Dakota, to Mankato, Mnisota.

The Memorial Riders travel 325 miles on horseback for eighteen days, sometimes through sub-zero blizzards.

They conclude their journey on December 26, the day of the hanging.

Memorials help focus our memory on particular people or events.

Often, memorials come in the forms of plaques, statues, or gravestones.

The memorial for the Dakota 38 is not an object inscribed with words, but an *act*.

Yet, I started this piece because I was interested in writing about grasses.

So, there is one other event to include, although it's not in chronological order and we must backtrack a little.

When the Dakota people were starving, as you may remember, government traders would not extend store credit to "Indians."

One trader named Andrew Myrick is famous for his refusal to provide credit to Dakota people by saying, "If they are hungry, let them eat grass."

There are variations of Myrick's words, but they are all something to that effect.

When settlers and traders were killed during the Sioux Uprising, one of the first to be executed by the Dakota was Andrew Myrick.

When Myrick's body was found,

                                        his mouth was stuffed with grass.

I am inclined to call this act by the Dakota warriors a poem.

There's irony in their poem.

There was no text.

"Real" poems do not "really" require words.

I have italicized the previous sentence to indicate inner dialogue, a revealing moment.

But, on second thought, the words "Let them eat grass" click the gears of the poem into place.

So, we could also say, language and word choice are crucial to the poem's work.

Things are circling back again.

Sometimes, when in a circle, if I wish to exit, I must leap.

And let the body   swing.

From the platform.

                              Out

                                        to the grasses.

V. ONE SINGING THING

Elegy

   For my father

I think by now the river must be thick
      with salmon. Late August, I imagine it

as it was that morning: drizzle needling
      the surface, mist at the banks like a net

settling around us—everything damp
      and shining. That morning, awkward

and heavy in our hip waders, we stalked
      into the current and found our places—

you upstream a few yards and out
      far deeper. You must remember how

the river seeped in over your boots
      and you grew heavier with that defeat.

All day I kept turning to watch you, how
      first you mimed our guide's casting

then cast your invisible line, slicing the sky
      between us; and later, rod in hand, how

you tried—again and again—to find
      that perfect arc, flight of an insect

skimming the river's surface. Perhaps
    you recall I cast my line and reeled in

two small trout we could not keep.
    Because I had to release them, I confess,

I thought about the past—working
    the hooks loose, the fish writhing

in my hands, each one slipping away
    before I could let go. I can tell you now

that I tried to take it all in, record it
    for an elegy I'd write—one day—

when the time came. Your daughter,
    I was that ruthless. What does it matter

if I tell you I *learned* to be? You kept casting
    your line, and when it did not come back

empty, it was tangled with mine. Some nights,
    dreaming, I step again into the small boat

that carried us out and watch the bank receding—
    my back to where I know we are headed.

Object Permanence
[For John]

We wake as if surprised the other is still there,
each petting the sheet to be sure.

How we have managed our way
to this bed—beholden to heat like dawn

indebted to light. Though we're not so self-
important as to think everything

has led to this, everything has led to this.
There's a name for the animal

love makes of us—named, I think,
like rain, for the sound it makes.

You are the animal after whom other animals
are named. Until there's none left to laugh,

days will start with the same startle
and end with caterpillars gorged on milkweed.

O, how we entertain the angels
with our brief animation. O,

how I'll miss you when we're dead.

Crowning

Now that knowing means nothing,
now that you are more born
than being, more awake
than awaited, since I've seen
your hair deep inside mother,
a glimpse, grass in late
winter, early spring, watching
your mother's pursed, throbbing,
purpled power, her pushing
you for one whole hour, two,
almost three, almost out,
maybe never, animal smell
and peat, breath and sweat
and mulch-matter, and at once
you descend, or drive, are driven
by mother's body, by her will
and brilliance, by bowel,
by wanting and your hair
peering as if it could see, and I saw
you storming forth,
taproot, your cap of hair half
in, half out, and *wait, hold
it there*, the doctors say, and
she squeezing my hand, her face
full of fire, then groaning your face
out like a flower, blood-bloom,
crocused into air, shoulders

and the long cord still rooting
you to each other, to the other
world, into this afterlife
among us living, the cord
I cut like an iris, pulsing,
then you wet against mother's chest
still purple, not blue, not yet
red, no cry,
warming now, now opening
your eyes midnight
blue in the blue black dawn.

Hurricane

Four tickets left, I let her go—
Firstborn into a hurricane.

I thought she escaped
The floodwaters. No—but her

Head is empty of the drowned
For now—though she took

Her first breath below sea level.
Ahhh   awe   &   aw
Mama, let me go—she speaks

What every smart child knows—
To get grown you unlatch

Your hands from the grown
& up & up & up & up
She turns—latched in the seat

Of a hurricane. (You let
Your girl what? You let

Your girl what?)
I did so she do I did
So she do so—

Girl, you can ride
A hurricane & she do
& she do & she do & she do

She do make my river
An ocean. Memorial.
Baptist. Protestant. Birth—my girl

Walked away from a hurricane.
& she do & she do & she do & she do
She do take my hand a while longer.

The haunts in my pocket
I'll keep to a hum: *Katrina was*
A woman I knew. When you were

An infant she rained on you & she

do & she do & she do & she do

Requiem for Fifth Period
   and the Things That Went On Then

Sing, muse, of the science teacher
looking wearily at the stack of ungraded projects
leaning against the back wall, beneath a board on which
she has hastily drawn a pinnate leaf and a palmate leaf
with a violet dry erase marker.
She moves from her desk to the window to watch the flag
      football game
and the man in the electric wheelchair leaving the senior housing
      complex
and an old Lincoln Town Car parked near the tremendous
      pothole that damaged her axle that morning
and the White Castle bag moving in a sudden gust across the
      basketball court, as if possessed
and Mr. Harris, blowing his whistle.

Tell us of Javonte Stevens, who is in the fourth grade
and who is now tapping Mr. Harris on the shoulder to say
that Miss Kaizer will be sending over three kids
who did not bring in their field trip money
and cannot go to the aquarium
and is that okay.
Sing of Javonte's new glasses,
their black frames and golden hinges that glint in the sun,
and his new haircut, with two notched arrows shorn above his
      temples

and his new socks which are hidden but which feel best of all
and which were the last of the new things he received from his
    auntie this weekend
when she visited from Detroit and slept on the couch and
    declared that
Javonte's improved grades meant that he should have many new
    things.
Sing of the rough-hewn piece of wood Javonte used
to keep the heavy door ajar while he was outside.
Call out
the noise it made against the painted cement when he kicked it
    back in.
Sing the song Javonte hummed as he carried his message
back up the stairs, stepping in tune, nodding in tune
to Bo as she called after him,
warning him not to slip on the newly mopped floor.

Sing, muse, of Bo, moving the mop
from the top of the ramp to the bottom,
stepping gingerly past the place where the carpet's unruly corner
    bends upward,
guiding the wheels of the bucket to stay unwillingly upright
despite the heavy dent in the one.
Speak of the pungent, alkaline smell of the water
and the slap when the fibers hit the floor
and the squeal of the bathroom door
and the shuddering sob,
audible in the moment that disc two of *The Broker* by John Grisham

skips in Bo's CD player,
and her pause in the threshold
and her retreat to the boys' room, which can be cleaned first.

Tell of Nakyla Smith, breathing in sharply when the bathroom
   door closes,
pushing the stall open gently, silently moving to the sink,
splashing water on her face and wiping her eyes
with the sleeve of her blue oxford.
Sing of her heavy ascent to the counselor's office,
for today is the day
she will unbutton her collar, and the button below, and the
   button below,
and tug aside the bleached white tank top
to show the small, round burns that pepper her breast.
Praise Ms. Hightower, who does not gasp or cry out at the
   moment of revelation,
only holds one brown hand in her own
and with her left, lifts the phone and dials Mrs. Marshall,
though she is only just across the hall.

Sing, muse, of Mrs. Marshall, who cannot answer now.
The desk is unattended and she leans
against the other side of the oaken door,
the principal's side, where a sign reads "Children Are My Business"
and a doll-like painted woman smiles broadly, surrounded by the
   faces of earnest pupils.
She is resting against the wood as her forearms strain
with the weight of all the papers,

colored like oatmeal or dust, each with a label at the top.
The first says STEVENS, JAVONTE, and below that, KAIZER,
and below that, eight numbers.
Tell of how she collates them by classroom, then alphabetically,
though each letter is the same, though each bears the same news.

Tell, muse, of the siren that called their joy sparse and their love
    vacant.
Tell of the wind that scattered them.

Dear P.

Someone will   love you   many will   love

you   many will brother you   some of these

loves will   bother you   some   will   leave you

one might   haunt   you   hunt you in your

sleep   make you   weep the tearless kind of

weep the   kind of weep   that drowns your

organs   slowly   there are little oars   in your body

little boats   grab onto them and row and   row

someone will tell you   *no*   but you won't   know

he is   right until you have   already   wrung your

own heart dry   your hands dripping knives   until

you have   already   reached your hands into   his

body and put them through his   heart   love is

the only thing that   is not   an   argument

Lines for Little Mila

Here, in a cloud of rising flour
she dabs at her chin—   aging
leaves a blemish just like this . . .
the egg behind the cloud
of flour now falling
to a black mica counter.

Grandmother with a coffee tin
full of raw milk. The sun
gone beyond the mountains
long before it's gone from us.

Men cleaning fish, husking
corn on the porch.

I told a friend's little girl
about some of this,
and she immediately
slumbered, putting
a blue ghost inside my chest.

I said to her—
so you still remember things from the other side?
Then quickly I added—

of that river?

Mercy

Like two wrestlers etched
around some ancient urn

we'd lace our hands,
then wrench

each other's wrists back
until the muscles ached

and the tendons burned,
and one brother

or the other grunted *Mercy*—
a game we played

so many times
I finally taught my sons,

not knowing what it was,
until too late, I'd done:

when the oldest rose
like my brother's ghost,

grappling the little
ghost I was at ten—

who cried out *Mercy!*
in my own voice *Mercy!*

as I watched from deep
inside my father's skin.

Apparition

I'm carrying an orange plastic basket of compost
down from the top of the garden—sweet dark,

fibrous rot, promising—when the light changes
as if someone's flipped a switch that does

what? Reverses the day. Leaves chorusing,
dizzy. And then my mother says

—she's been gone more than thirty years,
not her voice, the voice of her in me—

You've got to forgive me. I'm choke and sputter
in the wild daylight, speechless to that:

maybe I'm really crazy now, but I believe
in the backwards morning I am my mother's son,

we are at last equally in love
with intoxication, I am unregenerate,

the trees are on fire, fifty-eight years of lost bells.
I drop my basket and stand struck

in the iron-mouth afternoon. She says
I never meant to harm you. Then

the young dog barks, down by the front gate,
he's probably gotten out, and she says,

calmly, clearly, *Go take care of your baby.*

At Pegasus

They are like those crazy women
    who tore Orpheus
        when he refused to sing,

these men grinding
    in the strobe & black lights
        of Pegasus. All shadow & sound.

"I'm just here for the music,"
    I tell the man who asks me
        to the floor. But I have held

a boy on my back before.
    Curtis & I used to leap
        barefoot into the creek; dance

among maggots & piss,
    beer bottles & tadpoles
        slippery as sperm;

we used to pull off our shirts,
    & slap music into our skin.
        He wouldn't know me now

at the edge of these lovers' gyre,
    glitter & steam, fire,
        bodies blurred sexless

by the music's spinning light.
    A young man slips his thumb
        into the mouth of an old one,

& I am not that far away.
    The whole scene raw & delicate
        as Curtis's foot gashed

on a sunken bottle shard.
    They press hip to hip,
        each breathless as a boy

carrying a friend on his back.
    The foot swelling green
        as the sewage in that creek.

We never went back.
    But I remember his weight
        better than I remember

my first kiss.
    These men know something
        I used to know.

How could I not find them
    beautiful, the way they dive & spill
        into each other,

the way the dance floor
    takes them,
        wet & holy in its mouth.

Scorch Marks

Whenever we find wide black swaths burned across our paths
We think of you. Our friend the black swan turns to look
At us frequently when we pass by its pond. We see your back
Far away deep inside the pupils of those we love. We stare
And we stare where we are. That is what we do. It makes us
Look as if we've misplaced our minds or perhaps replaced
Ideas of mind with some new stronger fog. I feel you
Fading and find you falling for that feeling, you staring farther
Into one of the farthest vanishing points in the universe.
We find this alarming. We are losing track of something.
Our friend the black dog watches us carefully as we walk by
The door she guards. The crows look at us in their crooked
Ways. They converse and inverse and walk like the mechanics
Of mystery they are. Who are we to believe what we say?

Dog Talk

We-be bo-broke e-bev-ry-by
sy-byl-la-ba-ble-ble

O-bour mo-bouths bo-broke the-bem
an-band o-bo-pe-bened the-bem
fo-bor ai-bair o-bor wa-ba-ter-ber
o-bor see-beed o-bot foo-bood.

A-banse-se-bers, que-bues-tio-bens,
na-bames, se-be-cre-bets. We-be
be-bent E-ben-gli-bish,
em-bern-bra-baced i-bit
the-ben e-be-ra-based i-bit
a-bat the-be sa-bame ti-bime.

Romanticism 101

Then I realized I hadn't secured the boat.
Then I realized my friend had lied to me.
Then I realized my dog was gone
no matter how much I called in the rain.
All was change.
Then I realized I was surrounded by aliens
disguised as orthodontists having a convention
at the hotel breakfast bar.
Then I could see into the life of things,
that systems seek only to reproduce
the conditions of their own reproduction.
If I had to pick between shadows
and essences, I'd pick shadows.
They're better dancers.
They always sing their telegrams.
Their old gods do not die.
Then I realized the very futility was salvation
in this greeny entanglement of breaths.
Yeah, as if.
Then I realized even when you catch the mechanism,
the trick still convinces.
Then I came to in Texas
and realized rockabilly would never go away.
Then I realized I'd been drugged.
We were all chasing nothing
which left no choice but to intensify the chase.
I came to handcuffed and gagged.

I came to intubated and packed in some kind of foam.
This too is how ash moves through water.
And all this time the side door unlocked.
Then I realized repetition could be an ending.
Then I realized repetition could be an ending.

For the Last American Buffalo
After a photograph by Richard Sherman

Because words dazzle in the dizzy light of things
and the soul is like an animal—hunted and slow—
this buffalo walks through me every night as if I was
some kind of prairie and hunkers against the cold dark,
snorting under the stars while the fog of its breathing
rises in the air, and it is the loneliest feeling I know
to approach it slowly with my hand outstretched
to tenderly touch the heavy skull furred and rough
and stroke that place huge between its ears where
what I think and what it thinks are one singing thing
so quiet that, when I wake, I seldom remember
walking beside it and whispering in its ear quietly
passing the miles, the two of us, as if Cheyenne or
the lights of San Francisco were our unlikely destination
and sometimes trains pass us and no one leans out hard
in the dark aiming to end us and so we continue on
somehow and today while the seismic quietness of
the earth spun beneath my feet and while the world
I guess carried on, that lumbering thing moved heavy
thick and dark through the dreams I believe we keep
having whether we sleep or not and when you see it
again say *I'm sorry* for things you didn't do and
then offer it some sweet-grass and tell it stories
you remember from the star-chamber of the womb
or at least the latest joke, something good to keep it
company as otherwise it doesn't know you are here
for love, and like the world tonight, doesn't really
care whether we live or die. Tell it you do and why.

JAN BEATTY is the author of *Jackknife: New and Selected Poems*, and was named by the *Huffington Post* as one of ten women writers for "required reading." She lives in Pittsburgh, Pennsylvania.

JERICHO BROWN is the author of *The New Testament* and *Please*. He teaches in the creative writing program at Emory University and lives in Atlanta, Georgia.

TINA CHANG is the author of *Half-Lit Houses* and *Of Gods & Strangers*, and is coeditor of *Language for a New Century: Contemporary Poetry from the Middle East, Asia, and Beyond*. She lives in Brooklyn, New York.

VICTORIA CHANG's poetry collections include *Circle*, *Salvinia Molesta*, *The Boss*, and *Barbie Chang*. She lives in Southern California.

OLIVER DE LA PAZ is the author of four poetry collections, *Names above Houses*, *Furious Lullaby*, *Requiem for the Orchard*, and *Post Subject: A Fable*. He teaches at the College of the Holy Cross and in the low-residency MFA program at Pacific Lutheran University. He lives in Massachusetts.

NATALIE DIAZ was born and raised in the Fort Mojave Indian Village in Needles, California. She is Mojave and an enrolled member of the Gila River Indian Tribe. Diaz teaches at Arizona State University, and her first poetry collection is *When My Brother Was an Aztec*.

MATTHEW DICKMAN is the author of *All-American Poem*, *Mayakovsky's Revolver*, and *Wonderland*. He lives in Portland, Oregon.

MARK DOTY is a poet, essayist, and memoirist. He is the author of ten books of poetry, including *Deep Lane* and *Fire to Fire: New and Selected Poems*, which won the National Book Award. He lives in New York, New York.

NORMAN DUBIE is the author of twenty-eight collections of poetry, most recently *The Quotations of Bone*, which won the Griffin Poetry Prize. He lives and teaches in Tempe, Arizona.

JEHANNE DUBROW is the author of six books of poetry, including *Dots & Dashes, Red Army Red*, and *Stateside*. She is an associate professor of creative writing at the University of North Texas.

EVE L. EWING is a poet, essayist, sociologist, and educator. *Electric Arches* is her first book of poetry. She lives in Chicago, Illinois.

VIEVEE FRANCIS is the author of *Blue-Tail Fly, Horse in the Dark*, and *Forest Primeval*, which won the Kingsley Tufts Poetry Award and the Hurston/Wright Legacy Award in Poetry. She teaches at Dartmouth College.

ROSS GAY is the author of *Catalog of Unabashed Gratitude*, winner of the National Book Critics Circle Award and the Kingsley Tufts Poetry Award. He teaches at Indiana University.

ARACELIS GIRMAY is the author of three collections of poetry, including *Teeth, Kingdom Animalia*, and *The Black Maria*. Originally from California, she lives with her family in New York, New York.

NATHALIE HANDAL is the author of five books of poetry, including *The Republics* and *Poet in Andalucía*. She is a professor at Columbia University and lives in New York, New York.

JOY HARJO is the author of eight books of poetry, most recently *Conflict Resolution for Holy Beings*. She was recently awarded the Ruth Lilly Prize for lifetime achievement in poetry from the Poetry Foundation. She is a member of the Muscogee Nation and teaches at the University of Tennessee.

YONA HARVEY is the author of *Hemming the Water*, which won the Kate Tufts Discovery Award. She teaches at the University of Pittsburgh.

TERRANCE HAYES is the author of six poetry collections, including *American Sonnets for My Past and Future Assassin, How to Be Drawn*, and *Lighthead*, which won the National Book Award. He is a MacArthur Fellow and teaches at the University of Pittsburgh.

CATHY PARK HONG is a poet and critic whose books include *Translating Mo'um*, *Dance Dance Revolution*, and *Engine Empire*. She is a professor at Rutgers–Newark University.

MARIE HOWE is the author of four books of poetry, including *Magdalene* and *What the Living Do*. She lives in New York, New York.

MAJOR JACKSON is the author of four collections of poetry, *Roll Deep*, *Holding Company*, *Hoops*, and *Leaving Saturn*. He teaches at the University of Vermont.

ILYA KAMINSKY was born in the former Soviet Union and is now an American citizen. He is the author of two poetry books, *Deaf Republic* and *Dancing in Odessa*, and editor of *The Ecco Anthology of International Poetry*. He received a Whiting Writers' Award. He teaches at San Diego State University.

LAURA KASISCHKE teaches in the MFA program at the University of Michigan. She is the author of many books of poetry, including *Where Now: New and Selected Poems* and *Space, in Chains*, which won the National Book Critics Circle Award in Poetry. She lives in Ann Arbor, Michigan.

DONIKA KELLY's first poetry collection is *Bestiary*, winner of the Cave Canem Poetry Prize and the Kate Tufts Discovery Award. She lives in Brooklyn, New York.

ROBIN COSTE LEWIS's first book of poems, *Voyage of the Sable Venus*, won the National Book Award in Poetry. She lives and teaches in Los Angeles, California.

ADA LIMÓN is the author of five books of poetry, including *The Carrying* and *Bright Dead Things*, which was a finalist for the National Book Award. She lives in Lexington, Kentucky, and Sonoma, California.

PATRICIA LOCKWOOD is the author of two books of poetry, *Motherland Fatherland Homelandsexuals* and *Balloon Pop Outlaw Black*, and a memoir, *Priestdaddy*. She lives in Savannah, Georgia.

LAYLI LONG SOLDIER is the author of *WHEREAS*, which won the National Book Critics Circle Award and the PEN/Jean Stein Award and was a finalist for the National Book Award. She is a citizen of the Oglala Lakota Nation and lives in Santa Fe, New Mexico.

PATRICK PHILLIPS is the author of *Chattahoochee*, *Boy*, and *Elegy for a Broken Machine*, which was a finalist for the National Book Award. He lives in Brooklyn, New York.

LIA PURPURA's latest poetry collection is *It Shouldn't Have Been Beautiful*. The recipient of a Guggenheim fellowship and a finalist for the National Book Critics Circle Award, she teaches at the University of Maryland and lives in Baltimore, Maryland.

MELISSA RANGE is the author of *Horse and Rider* and *Scriptorium*. Originally from East Tennessee, she now lives in Wisconsin and teaches at Lawrence University.

MATT RASMUSSEN is the author of *Black Aperture*, winner of the Walt Whitman Award of the Academy of American Poets and a finalist for the National Book Award. He lives in Robbinsdale, Minnesota.

ERIKA L. SÁNCHEZ is the author of a poetry collection, *Lessons on Expulsion*, and a novel for young readers, *I Am Not Your Perfect Mexican Daughter*, which was a finalist for the National Book Award. She lives in Chicago, Illinois.

STEVE SCAFIDI is the author of four poetry collections, including *Sparks from a Nine-Pound Hammer* and *To the Bramble and the Briar*. He lives in Summit Point, West Virginia.

NICOLE SEALEY is the author of *Ordinary Beast* and *The Animal After Whom Other Animals Are Named*. She is the executive director of Cave Canem and lives in Brooklyn, New York.

CHARIF SHANAHAN's first poetry collection is *Into Each Room We Enter without Knowing*. He is a Stegner Fellow at Stanford University and lives in the Bay Area of California.

SOLMAZ SHARIF is the author of a poetry collection, *Look*, a finalist for the National Book Award. She is currently a lecturer at Stanford University and lives in the Bay Area of California.

DANEZ SMITH is the author of two books of poetry, *[insert] boy* and *Don't Call Us Dead*, a finalist for the National Book Award. They live in Minneapolis, Minnesota.

SUSAN STEWART is the author of six books of criticism and six collections of poetry, including *Cinder: New and Selected Poems* and *Columbarium*, which won the National Book Critics Circle Award. She teaches at Princeton University and lives in New Jersey and in Philadelphia, Pennsylvania.

MARY SZYBIST is the author of two poetry collections, *Granted* and *Incarnadine*, which won the National Book Award. She teaches at Lewis & Clark College and lives in Portland, Oregon.

NATASHA TRETHEWEY is the author of four collections of poetry, including *Thrall* and *Native Guard*, which won the Pulitzer Prize. She served as the nineteenth Poet Laureate of the United States from 2012 to 2014. She is Board of Trustees Professor at Northwestern University and lives in Evanston, Illinois.

BRIAN TURNER is a veteran of the United States Army and the author of the poetry collections *Phantom Noise* and *Here, Bullet*, as well as the memoir *My Life as a Foreign Country*. He lives in Orlando, Florida.

ELLEN BRYANT VOIGT is the author of eight collections of poetry, including *Headwaters* and *Messenger: New and Selected Poems*, which was a finalist for the National Book Award and the Pulitzer Prize. She is a MacArthur Fellow and lives in Cabot, Vermont.

SUSAN WHEELER is the author of six collections of poetry, including *Assorted Poems* and *Meme*, which was a finalist for the National Book Award. She teaches in the Creative Writing Program at Princeton University.

DARA WIER is the author of fifteen collections of poetry, including *You Good Thing* and *Selected Poems*. She is the director of the MFA Program at the University of Massachusetts, Amherst.

CHRISTIAN WIMAN is a poet, translator, and essayist. His books of poetry include *Every Riven Thing* and *Once in the West*, which was a finalist for the National Book Critics Circle Award. He teaches at Yale University and lives in New Haven, Connecticut.

CHARLES WRIGHT was named Poet Laureate of the United States in 2014. He is the author of numerous collections of poetry, including *Bye-and-Bye: Selected Late Poems*. He taught at the University of Virginia.

JOHN YAU has published more than fifty books of poetry, fiction, and art criticism, including *A Thing among Things: The Art of Jasper Johns* and *Bijoux in the Dark*. He teaches at the Mason Gross School of the Arts (Rutgers University), and lives in New York, New York.

DEAN YOUNG is the author of many collections of poetry, including *Shock by Shock*, *Bender: New and Selected Poems*, and *Elegy on a Toy Piano*, a finalist for the Pulitzer Prize. He teaches at the University of Texas, Austin.

KEVIN YOUNG is director of The New York Public Library's Schomburg Center for Research in Black Culture and poetry editor of the *New Yorker*. He is the author of thirteen books of poetry and prose, including *Brown*, *Blue Laws: Selected & Uncollected Poems 1995–2015*, *Bunk*, a finalist for the National Book Critics Circle Award in criticism, and *Jelly Roll*, a finalist for the National Book Award in poetry.

119

ABOUT TRACY K. SMITH

TRACY K. SMITH is the Poet Laureate of the United States. She is the author of four collections of poetry, including *Wade in the Water* and *Life on Mars*, winner of the Pulitzer Prize. She is also the author of a memoir, *Ordinary Light*, which was a finalist for the National Book Award. She teaches at Princeton University and lives in New Jersey.

The text of *American Journal* is set in Adobe Caslon Pro. Book design by Rachel Holscher. Composition by Bookmobile Design & Digital Publisher Services, Minneapolis, Minnesota. Manufactured by Friesens on acid-free, 100 percent postconsumer wastepaper.

9284